372.21

Nature,
Living and
Growing

Ready, Steady, Play!

Series Editor: Sandy Green

Guaranteed fun for children and practitioners alike, the Ready, Steady, Play! series provides lively and stimulating activities for children.

Each book focuses on one specific aspect of play offering clear and detailed guidance on how to plan and enjoy wonderful play experiences with minimum fuss and maximum success.

Each book in the Ready, Steady, Play! series includes advice on:

- How to prepare the children and the play space
- What equipment and materials are needed
- How much time is needed to prepare and carry out the activity
- How many staff are required
- How to communicate with parents and colleagues

Ready, Steady, Play! helps you to:

- Develop activities easily, using suggested guidelines
- Ensure that health and safety issues are taken into account
- Plan play that links to the early years curriculum
- Broaden your understanding of early years issues

Early years practitioners and students on early years courses and parents looking for simple, excellent ideas for creative play will love these books!

Other titles in the series

Books, Stories and Puppets 1-84312-148-4 Green
Construction 1-84312-098-4 Boyd
Creativity 1-84312-076-3 Green
Displays and Interest Tables 1-84312-267-7 Olpin
Festivals 1-84312-101-8 Hewitson
Food and Cooking 1-84312-100-X Green
Music and Singing 1-84312-276-6 Durno
Play Using Natural Materials 1-84312-099-2 Howe
Role Play 1-84312-147-6 Green

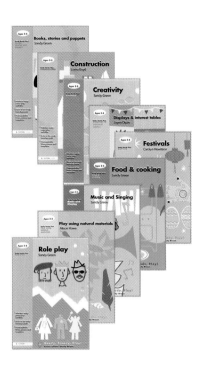

Nature, Living and Growing

Sue Harper

David Fulton Publishers

David Fulton Publishers Ltd
The Chiswick Centre, 414 Chiswick High Road, London W4 5TF

www.fultonpublishers.co.uk

First published in Great Britain in 2005 by David Fulton Publishers

10 9 8 7 6 5 4 3 2 1

Note: The right of Sue Harper to be identified as the author of this work has been asserted by her in accordance with the Copyright, Designs and Patents Act 1988.

David Fulton Publishers is a division of Granada Learning Limited, part of ITV plc.

British Library Cataloguing in Publication Data
A catalogue record for this book is available from the British Library.

ISBN 1-84312-114-X

Typeset by FiSH Books, London
Printed and bound in Great Britain

Contents

Nature, Living and Growing

Welcome to *Nature, Living and Growing*, an exciting new publication which is part of the Ready, Steady, Play! series.

Get ready to enjoy a range of activities with your children, which will stimulate their all-round development.

The Ready, Steady, Play! books will help boost the confidence of new practitioners by providing informative and fun ideas to support planning and preparation. The series will also consolidate and extend learning for the more experienced practitioner. Attention is drawn to health and safety, and the role of the adult is addressed.

How to use this book

Nature, Living and Growing is divided into four main sections.

The Introduction sets out background information regarding why working with nature provides such wonderful experiences for young children. It offers useful tips to keep in mind as the seasons progress, and addresses both health and safety issues and the role of the adult.

The second section, 'Discussion resources', presents visual material to stimulate discussion with children, broadening their knowledge of their environment, both local and further afield.

The Activities section has been divided into the four seasons of the year, spring, summer, autumn and winter, beginning with autumn, the first season of the academic year. Each season has a 'season specific' introduction, followed by six activities. The activities have been chosen to reflect the mood of each season and the resources available at that particular time of year.

Finally, the 'Photocopiable pages' section provides related activities for children to enjoy and complete. These pages build on the learning aims of the set activities, or follow on from the 'Discussion resources' section, and may be used as evidence of developing skills and understanding, or to involve parents in what their child has been learning.

So read on, and enjoy ... Ready, Steady, Play!

Sandy Green
Series editor

Acknowledgements

Many thanks to my colleagues in the early years team, head teacher, parents and children of St Saviour's Nursery and Infant School, Bath, for their encouragement and support and for granting permission for use of photographic material.

To Sandy Green, the series editor, whose IT skills, time and patience ensured my book made publication.

Thanks also to Insect Lore for the use of their photos.

Series acknowledgement

The series editor would like to thank the children, parents and staff at:

- The Nursery and Reception class, Wadebridge Community Primary School, Wadebridge, Cornwall
- Happy Days Day Nursery, Wadebridge, Cornwall
- Snapdragons Nursery, Weston, Bath, Somerset
- Snapdragons Nursery, Grosvenor, Bath, Somerset
- Tadpoles Nursery, Combe Down, Bath, Somerset

for allowing us to take photographs of their excellent provision, resources and displays.

Also to John and Jake Green, Jasmine and Eva for their help throughout the series.

Introduction

In the early 1990s, we and our four children took a huge gamble and swapped the security and comfort of suburban Bristol and secure employment, for a 70-acre wood and farm. The buildings were almost derelict, and having little knowledge of house renovation on such a major scale, and even less of stock keeping and land management, a whole new learning process evolved for us all. The children, who had had very little contact with the countryside, took to their new way of life like 'ducks to water'.

Coupled with this transformation, and to help keep us financially afloat, I restarted a career as an Early Years Educator and secured a position in the Nursery class of an Infant School in Bath.

As my observations, skills and love of nature developed, I began sharing it with the children in school with positive results. Class visits to the wood were hugely popular. Young children are instinctively curious about their natural surroundings, and the freedom to explore such a huge outdoor natural resource awakened their sense of curiosity, wonder and creativity.

With no other resources other than the ones nature provides, children spent hours building dens from branches and odd-shaped tree trunks, constructed bridges over the stream from fallen logs, making it strong enough to walk over; made mud cakes from the 'swampy bit', collected clay from the bed of the stream and, using their hands, spread it over logs and branches. They tested their strength and took risks in tree- and rock-climbing, collected wild garlic, found spiders' nests, collected materials for the bonfire, got wet and very muddy and didn't seem to care!

Nature provides huge play opportunities, not only for exploring and investigating, but for creativity, developing language and communication skills, assessing risk, increasing sensory awareness, teamwork, resourcefulness and ultimately feeling an empathy with the natural world.

I fully appreciate that not all settings will have access to such a unique provision as a wood, yet opportunities still exist whereby children can be given the chance to share in their outdoor natural world. The changing seasons, weather, growth, life processes and cycles, carry on regardless, outside every front door: in garden tubs, roadside bushes, shrubs, trees, parks, hedgerows, wasteland, public footpaths, fields or a neighbour's garden. Nature is always out there, doing what it needs to do to survive all year round.

So wherever or whatever the restrictions or limitations to outdoors that your setting imposes, you and your children can experience the magic and wonder of nature and take it inside to your classrooms and play areas.

The aim of this book, therefore, is to help practitioners and children keep in touch with their outdoor world in a simple, creative and achievable way. I aim to raise the profile of nature and to present it as an exciting, ongoing and easily available all-year-round resource, for extending child development through all areas of the Foundation Stage Curriculum.

Through their play and investigations, children's growing awareness, knowledge and respect for their natural environment and how things live and grow, will increase. This will then give rise to a greater understanding, empathy and appreciation of the unique and valuable role nature plays within their world.

Remember

- Encourage the children outside, whatever the weather; they'll learn more about nature outside the setting than in.

- When outside, adopt the role of guide, a provider of opportunities for learning, rather than an instructor of names and facts.

- Encourage children to observe and use their senses – observation is the first step to understanding nature.

- Provide thought-provoking questions that prompt children to consider aspects of their outdoor natural environment. For example: How different are our needs to those of our wildlife. Are they the same or similar? What would happen if there were no trees?

- Ensure children are adequately dressed for any outdoor walk or investigation, appropriate to the weather/season. There is no such thing as bad weather, only the wrong clothes.

- In any outdoor opportunity, be receptive. Nature can sometimes 'kindle' an enthusiasm in a child which can then be skilfully led towards learning. It is important that children be allowed to discover a meaningful experience for themselves.

- As a practitioner, be aware of what's happening outside; nature always provides something interesting or exciting to explore – a bird singing sweetly, a frog hopping across the grass, a squirrel on the bird table, a wild wind blowing. Let the children experience it first and talk about it after.

- Don't worry if you don't know all the answers, it's not important. There is more to an oak tree than a load of facts and figures: the feel of its bark, the sound of the rustling leaves, the birds and insects that live in it, and so on.

- Bring natural products into the class/playroom, such as large stones, pebbles, logs, bark, pine cones, conkers, branches, twigs. Add them to areas of your setting for children to freely access, for example in small world, sand, water or role play.

- A camera is useful to photograph children and their observations. Making a note of their involvement/observations/comments will also add real meaning to their play and can also provide practitioners with a useful focal or starting-point, for an area of learning, activity or display.

Equipment and resources

Useful items to have around would include:

■ Magnifying glasses for close observation.

■ Small clear plastic containers for insect gathering – always pierce a few holes in the top to enable insects to breathe.

N.B. *It is important to release insects back into the wild as soon as children lose interest.*

■ Binoculars for viewing birds, squirrels, etc. at a distance.

■ Wind chimes to help gauge weather.

■ Clay and soil can be used in many 'nature' activities.

■ Branches, logs and tree stumps are ideal for exploring natural insect and plant life. (Try asking for unwanted material when you see pruning or tree-cutting taking place.)

Health and safety

Attention to health and safety is vital when working in the outdoor environment. Relevant points to consider have been indicated for each of the activities in this book. A summary of these points is as follows:

- Adult to carry out a risk assessment in advance of each activity.
- Adult awareness is needed of poisonous plants (see examples below), and children must be taught not to touch plant material without adult agreement.
- Ensure that children wash their hands thoroughly after any contact with insects, soil and any other materials of concern.
- Always maintain appropriate adult : child ratios.
- Request sun hats and use of sun block when working out of doors in hot weather.
- Carefully supervise use of all sharp implements (e.g. knives, trowels, forks, etc.).
- Limit numbers when closer supervision is needed (such as when using sharp implements).
- Be aware of allergies, and plan in advance to provide alternative arrangements or activities for affected children.
- Remember that the cooker should only be used by the adult.

Examples of commonly found poisonous plants

Yew – the berries are poisonous

Arum

Green potatoes

Laburnum

Foxglove

Elder – the raw berries are poisonous

Many types of fungi

Autumn crocus

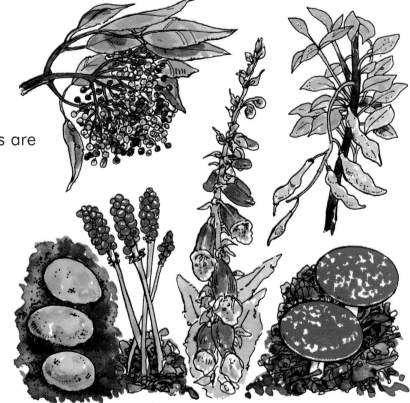

Remember

Never eat anything unless you are sure it is safe to do so. Wash hands thoroughly if anything suspicious is touched accidentally.

The adult role

As well as ensuring a healthy and safe environment during 'nature' activities, the adult has other important roles too. These include:

- Planning activities carefully, ensuring that equality of opportunity is considered throughout.
- Enabling children to learn through exploration and investigation.
- Providing appropriate and sufficient resources for each activity, to ensure a satisfactory experience is gained by the children.
- Supporting learning through challenge and stimulation.
- Giving encouragement and praise.
- Helping to develop language use and vocabulary extension through discussion and questioning.
- Extending activities as appropriate.

Top Tips to support you in introducing nature to your children

1. Grow an acorn tree – Soak an acorn in warm water for several hours. Peel off the hard outer shell. Place a few stones in the base of a pot and fill with some soil and/or compost. Place the acorn on the top and cover with more soil. Lightly sprinkle with soil and put a plastic bag on the top and secure with string or an elastic band (this will keep the seed moist without watering it). Put it in a sunny spot indoors and wait until the little seedling appears. Remove the plastic bag and water once or twice a week. In the summer, place it outside and in the autumn plant it in the ground.

2. Bring in a few winter buds from broad-leaved trees, such as horse chestnut, ash, beech. Cut the twigs with scissors (do not break them). Put them into a jam jar or vase and place in a sunny position, and wait for the buds to open. This may take several weeks. Encourage the children to draw them.

3. Place a stick of celery or a white carnation into a jar of coloured water (cut the tips from the base to allow the flower or vegetable to drink). After a few hours children will be able to see that the water travels up the stem.

4. Encourage older children to sketch insects and other wildlife where they see them instead of always bringing them back to the setting.

5. Butterflies such as the peacock and tortoiseshell lay their eggs on stinging nettles. Encourage nettles to grow in your garden area so that when their eggs hatch, the caterpillars can survive by eating the leaves and the children can watch them with wonder.

6. Sow wild flower seeds in tubs or a window box. They will attract birds and insects.

7. On cold winter days, provide nutmeg graters and whole nutmegs. Children soon master how to use them and enjoy the activity. They love the smell and will enjoy collecting it into small pots.

8. Put small tubs or containers of water outside, to see if it freezes.

9. Tree cones can help you forecast the weather. When it is warm, the scales open up, but when a storm is on its way, they close up. To keep the seeds dry and make it open, place near a radiator. To make it close, place in a damp area.

10. In spring or summer, place pebbles or chalk around a puddle of water. How long does it take to disappear or evaporate?

11. To attract mini-beasts to your garden area, provide a small site with some old rotting logs and/or a tree stump, stones, etc. As the log pile rots, fungi will start to grow on it. Nettles and other flowering weeds may seed themselves there, which will attract flying insects, such as butterflies.

12. Slugs love beer! So, to stop them eating your plants, sink a dish of beer into the ground. The slugs will fall in, leaving your plants alone. Surround your plants with broken egg shells – snails will avoid moving over sharp areas.

13. To collect and observe insects, make a harmless insect trap by pushing a cup or jar into the ground so that the top is level with the ground. Put some bait inside, such as pieces of apple, cheese or meat. Lay a small stone either side of the jar, with a flat stone over the top. Leave overnight. What insects have been collected?

    N.B. *After studying them, return them to their natural habitat.*

14. Avoid using chemical sprays. They not only destroy the pest, such as greenfly, but kill off good insects too, including ladybirds and bees. Give plants a good soapy soaking from a spray bottle instead.

Remember

Ladybirds, hedgehogs, frogs and toads all eat harmful insects and do not damage your plants.

Discussion resources

The following section provides a range of photographs that can be used to stimulate discussion with children, broadening their knowledge of both their local and extended environment, and providing a starting-point for many activities involving nature.

Which seasons are these?

Which seasons are these?

Activities

The following pages contain twenty-four activities to enjoy throughout the year, divided into the four seasons. Each season has an introduction, and all the activities follow a standard format to ensure ease of planning and implementation:

- the resources needed
- the aim(s)/concept(s)
- the process
- group size
- health and safety
- vocabulary/discussion ideas
- extension ideas
- links to the Foundation Stage Curriculum.

Key to Foundation Stage Curriculum abbreviations:

(SS)   Stepping Stones

ELG Early Learning Goals

PSE Personal, social and emotional development

CLL Communication, language and literacy

MD Mathematical development

KUW Knowledge and understanding of the world

PD Physical development

CD Creative development

Introduction to autumn

For practitioners, encouraging children to enjoy their outdoor natural environment should be a central part of a routine, rather than an optional extra. Autumn is a great 'child friendly' season in which to put this into action.

On an autumn 'wonder walk', children's senses will be met with an array of beautiful colours, tastes, sights and sounds, and in this introduction are some ideas to take adults and children through this exciting season.

Autumn is the season when nature is preparing to 'shut down' for the winter, but before it does, it offers up all kinds of activities for us and our wildlife to explore.

- In autumn the days are shorter, nights are longer, colder and more windy. The sun rises later and sets earlier.
- The tops of the trees start to change colour, reds, yellows, browns and oranges. They make lovely rustling noises as they bend to and fro in the strong winds which roar through their

leaves, making them fall to the ground – fun to run through and collect. Some trees, like the horse chestnut and oak, make seeds for next year – conkers and acorns can be collected.

- Plants and trees spread their seeds in different ways. Encourage the children to look for seeds that are light enough to be blown by the wind, such as maple and dandelion. Explain that nature is helping the seeds to survive and that when they land on the soil, and if they survive the winter, the first few warm days of spring will wake them up, and a new plant or tree will prepare to grow. Nature is clever.

- Animals such as hedgehogs, badgers and dormice also prepare for winter and hibernate. They collect as many berries, nuts, seeds and fruit as they can and store them somewhere safe to eat during the cold winter months.

- Some birds, like the swallow, gather to migrate to warmer countries – look out for large flocks flying overhead.

- Some plants give us delicious berries to eat, like blackberries, fun to collect and eat raw or cooked. Birds and animals also love them.
  N.B. *Not all berries are safe for us to eat.*

- Autumn is traditionally considered to be harvest time. The fruits on our trees are ripe and ready for picking, like the apples, pears and damsons. Nuts from the hazel bush or tree can be collected and saved until they turn brown and are then ready for cracking open to eat. Pumpkins are ready to pick, to enjoy and to make lanterns with.

- Set up a seasonal table or display area where children can freely contribute with things they have collected or made and which can provide an ongoing focal area for autumn discussion.

Activities

1. Nature collage
2. Natural colour dyeing
3. Leaf banners
4. Bulb planting for a spring garden
5. Life in the soil: making a wormery
6. Pumpkin playtime

Worm facts

- They eat their own weight in organic matter every day.
- Worms often leave their back end in the burrow. If you touch them, they shoot back underground.
- Bristles on the worm's body grip in the soil, which sometimes makes it difficult for a bird to pull them out of the ground.
- A worm is both female and male. When they need to mate, they swap sperm to fertilise the eggs which they lay in the soil.
- Worms can live for several months or up to ten years.
- Some worms curl up and sleep when it is hot and dry in the summer.
- Moles store worms in an underground 'larder'. They bite off their heads to stop them escaping, but unless the mole eats it quickly, the worm can grow a new head and escape.
- Worms cannot live above ground. When dug up, they immediately burrow back into the soil.

Pumpkins

A pumpkin takes many months to grow. You can grow one either from seed or from a plant, and put it directly into the ground. When the plants have five leaves, pinch out the tips. This will make them bushy. They grow along the ground. Keep the fruits off the soil by laying them on straw or tiles (to avoid them being eaten by insects). Water the plant well throughout the summer. It will be ready in late autumn. Once picked, leave it to harden for two weeks before using.

ACTIVITY

1

Nature collage

Resources

- A selection from the following:
  - Wood shavings
  - Cereals such as oats
  - Small or broken shells
  - Sand
  - Seeds and beans
  - Herbs
  - Leaves
  - Feathers
  - Bits of bark/tiny twigs/pine needles/cones
  - Rounded pieces of sea glass
  - Small pieces of raffia or hessian
- Strong card (different sizes and shapes if liked)
- PVA glue and brushes
- Pencils

Aim/concept

To provide children with the opportunity to explore their environment and to consider what natural resources might be fun and interesting to use in creating a nature collage.

Process

In advance

- Discuss with the children ideas of natural resources that may be suitable for making a collage (select one or two as examples).
- Ask them to explore their environment both at home and within the setting to see what can be found.
- Provide card in various shapes and sizes.
- Display the selection of collected items, and explain to the children that they can choose their card and make a collage to their own design (they may wish to draw their idea first).
- Provide PVA glue.
- Encourage them to explore the different textures, talking about where they were found or where they came from.
- Supervise and support the children as they create their collages, admiring their work.

Vocabulary/discussion

- Name the different types of natural resources.
- Discuss the different textures and how they feel and smell.
- Talk about shape and size.
- Share stories as to where they found their particular resource.
- Did they have a favourite, which they preferred more than another? If so, why?

Group size

4–6

Extension ideas

1. Link the activity to a theme on nature/textures, etc.
2. Discuss similarities and differences between the resources.
3. Were some of the resources easier to stick to the card than others? If so, why?
4. Encourage children to extend their model-making/creative skills by making further use of the natural resources, e.g. painting patterns on twigs (snakes), making small boats by threading leaves onto small twigs, pushing them into clay and pressing into the base of walnut shells.

Links to Foundation Stage Curriculum

PSE	Show increasing independence in selecting and carrying out activities (SS)
ELG	Be confident to try new activities, initiate ideas and speak in a familiar group
CLL	Use talk, actions and objects to recall and relive past experiences (SS)
ELG	Use talk to organise, sequence and clarify thinking, ideas, feelings and events
MD	Show interest by sustained construction activity or by talking about shapes or arrangements (SS)
ELG	Talk about, recognise and recreate simple patterns
KUW	Explore objects (SS)
ELG	Look closely at similarities, differences, patterns and change
CD	Make constructions, collages, paintings, drawings and dances (SS)
ELG	Explore colour, texture, shape, form and space in two or three dimensions

Health and safety

⚠ Care to be taken with any sharp items.
⚠ Children to wash hands after the activity.

ACTIVITY 2 Natural colour dyeing

Resources

- Blackberries or raspberries
- Squares of white muslin or thin cotton
- Saucepan and saucers/plates
- Spoons, carrying container
- Small beads or pebbles, elastic bands
- Aprons
- To avoid staining, disposable table top cover

Aim/concept

To provide children with the opportunity to explore how the juice from fruit can be used as a natural dye to change the colour of cloth.

Process

- If possible, prior to the activity, take a walk with the children to pick and collect a few blackberries and discuss the difference between ripe and unripe fruit.
- Leave some uncooked for immediate colour dyeing investigation, and slightly cook others to release more juice. Allow to cool.
- Encourage children to describe their shape, colour and taste.
- Explain that the juice can be released by gently squeezing the blackberries directly onto the muslin/cloth. Alternatively, the fruit can be squeezed onto a plate and by either using their finger or a brush, the colour can be applied to the material to create a specific pattern.
- For a different impact and pattern effect, supervise the children as they wrap one, two or more beads/pebbles inside the square of cloth, securing them tightly with the elastic bands.
- Immerse the cloths into the softened and cooled blackberry juice and stir gently.
- Ask them what effect the beads/pebbles will have.
- Once the squares of cloth are well saturated, carefully remove from the pan and, carrying them carefully in a container, hang them out to dry.
- When dry, supervise the children as they remove the elastic bands and open up their coloured cloth.
- Ask them to describe what has happened and share in the enthusiasm of their discovery.

Vocabulary/discussion

- Discuss the fruits of autumn. What else can we pick at this time of year (e.g. apples)?
- Talk about the colour in nature.
- Discuss the difference in taste and appearance of the raw and cooked blackberries/raspberries.
- Share ideas on how the fruit can be cooked (either with or without apples) to make a delicious pudding, e.g. a pie or crumble, or a fruit smoothie.

Group size

4–6

Extension ideas

1. Link the activity to a topic/theme on food and/or seasons/festivals/harvest.
2. Provide cooking opportunities to allow for further enjoyment and exploration of the fruits of autumn, e.g. apple sauce.
3. Look more closely at the colours of autumn. What is happening outside at this time of year?
4. Discuss in more detail other fruits/vegetables which can be used to colour dye cloth, such as onion skins or beetroot.
5. Provide paint and opportunities for colour mixing, for children to create the colours of autumn.

Links to Foundation Stage Curriculum

KUW Talk about what is seen and what is happening (SS)

ELG Ask questions about why things happen and how things work

CD Respond to comments and questions, entering into dialogue about their creations (SS)

ELG Express and communicate their ideas, thoughts and feelings by using a widening range of materials, suitable tools, imaginative and role play, movement, designing and making, and a variety of songs and musical instruments

Health and safety

⚠ Take care when warming fruit. Allow to cool.

⚠ Beware of potential danger of beads/pebbles and elastic bands.

⚠ If blackberry picking, explain to the children to take care as the branches are prickly.

⚠ To avoid staining, aprons to be worn throughout activity and table to be covered.

⚠ Even after washing, hands still may be stained for a while after this activity. All part of the fun!!

⚠ Children prone to skin irritations may need to wear disposable gloves.

ACTIVITY

3 Leaf banners

Resources

- Approx. 8-inch squares of white/natural coloured muslin
- A selection of well-formed leaves, such as oak, horse chestnut, maple, beech, sycamore
- Old toothbrushes
- Selection of autumn colour poster/ready-made paints: yellow, red, brown, etc.
- Jar lids to use as paint containers
- Small half-inch round branches about 8 inches long
- Stapler
- Twine/hessian/string for hanging
- Pins for securing leaf to muslin

Aim/concept

To encourage children to observe the beautiful changes in leaf colour that take place at this time of year, and to collect a selection to create their own individual autumn banners.

Process

- If possible, prior to the activity, take the children to observe the changes in the autumn outdoor environment.
- Collect a selection of well-formed leaves, explaining they are to be used for creating a leaf print on a hanging banner.
- On the day of the activity, display the leaves and talk about their shape, size and colour.
- Ask children to choose a leaf and take a piece of muslin.
- Assist the children as they carefully pin the leaf to the cloth.
- Explain that there are a range of autumn colours to choose from in the jar lids.
- Using a toothbrush, demonstrate to the children that by dipping it into the colour and scraping it over the edge of the lid, the paint splatters all around the edge of the leaf.
- Ask them to think about the shape they will see when the leaf is removed.
- Encourage the children to experiment with a range/mix of colours, and supervise them as they create their prints.
- Carefully remove the leaf and share in their enthusiasm and wonder as they see its shape come to life. Allow to dry.
- Adult assistance may be needed in fixing the cloth over the branch with the stapler.
- Tie string/twine to each end of the branch for hanging and display.

Vocabulary/discussion

- Name the tree of which a leaf has been collected.
- Discuss the differences between the shape, size and colour of the leaves.
- Talk about what is happening to the trees and their leaves at this time of year.

Group size

4–6

Extension ideas

1. Link the activity to a theme on colour in the environment.
2. Encourage children to experiment with their own colour mixing to match the colours of autumn.
3. Encourage the children to collect and measure the appropriate length and diameter of twig for use with the banner.
4. Discuss in detail why leaves fall from the trees in autumn: the leaves are green because the sunshine helps the tree make chlorophyll (its food), but in autumn the chlorophyll in broad-leaved trees dies, therefore the leaves change colour and fall. The tree is preparing itself to sleep until spring.
5. Provide child-friendly resource books for further investigation on trees and environmental changes in the autumn season, e.g. weather, light, hibernation, and so on. For example, the Science through the Seasons series – *Autumn*, by Gabrielle Woolfitt, published by Wayland.

Links to Foundation Stage Curriculum

PSE	Display high levels of involvement in activities (SS)
ELG	Continue to be interested, excited and motivated to learn
CLL	Question why things happen and give explanations (SS)
ELG	Sustain attentive listening, responding to what they have heard by relevant comments, questions or actions
MD	Show curiosity and observation by talking about shapes, how they are the same or why some are different (SS)
ELG	Talk about, recognise and recreate simple patterns
PD	Demonstrate increasing skill and control in the use of mark-making implements, blocks and construction sets (SS)
ELG	Handle tools, objects, construction and malleable materials safely and with increasing control
CD	Choose particular colours to use for a purpose (SS)
ELG	Explore colour, texture, shape, form and space in two or three dimensions

Health and safety

⚠ Use only non-toxic paint.
⚠ Wash hands after leaf collection.
⚠ Care to be taken, or adult supervision, when using pins and stapler.

ACTIVITY 4 Bulb planting for a spring garden

Resources

- A selection of spring bulbs, e.g. daffodils, tulips, crocuses, snowdrops (with pictures)
- A container/containers/different sized flowerpots
- Compost
- Watering can, trowels
- Small stones/gravel for base of pot for water drainage

Aim/concept

Bulb planting in early autumn will help children to gain an understanding of how the cycle of seasons works.

Process

- Explain to the children that, once planted, the bulbs will rest in the sleeping earth until early spring, when their shoots push through, telling us that warmer weather is on the way.
- Ask the children to place small stones or gravel in the bottom of the container/pot, explaining that this helps the water to drain away.
- Using hands or trowel, encourage them to half fill the container with compost. The guide on page 85 may be helpful here.
- Using the pictures as examples, talk about the name, shape, colour and size of the different bulbs.
- Encourage thoughts and discussion about a planting design. For example, taller flowers at the back or in the centre, smaller ones at the front or around the edge. Single varieties and colour and/or a mix?
- Show the children which way up the bulb needs to be planted, explaining that the pointed end produces the growing shoot and the flat end produces the root.
- Supervise them as they place the bulbs close together (but not touching), into the container.

N.B. *As a general rule, plant bulbs twice as deep as their height.*

- Encourage the children to carefully cover the bulbs with more compost and to moisten with a little water.
- Decorate labels with the names of the different varieties planted.
- The pots can be placed either indoors or outdoors.
- Organise a watering schedule with the children, but do not saturate the bulbs as they will rot.

N.B. *When the bulbs have finished flowering, allow the plant to die back and go brown. In this way it is able to make food for next year's growth.*

Vocabulary/discussion

- Name the different bulb varieties, their colours, and different sizes.
- Using the pictures as a reference, which ones do they like best and why?
- Count the number being planted.
- Which bulbs do they think will pop up first?
- Discuss how through autumn, nature begins to 'shut down', to prepare for the long winter sleep: animals collect food for winter hibernation, flowers and plants die back, trees lose their leaves, and so

Group size

4–6

Extension ideas

1. Link to a theme/activity on planting and/or seasons.
2. Prior to planting, decorate plain coloured terracotta pots with poster paints.
3. When dry, apply a coat of clear varnish to stop the paint from running.
4. Let the children create their design on paper before planting.
5. Encourage children to write the names of each bulb variety on labels and to decorate.
6. Discuss in more detail the autumn season, observing any changes in temperature and hours of daylight, etc.

Links to Foundation Stage Curriculum

CLL Use writing as a means of recording and communicating (SS)

ELG Write their own names and other things such as labels and captions and begin to form simple sentences, sometimes using punctuation

MD Show an interest in shapes and space by playing with shapes or making arrangements with objects (SS)

ELG Use everyday words to describe position

KUW Begin to differentiate between past and present (SS)

ELG Find out about past and present events in their own lives, and those of their families and other people they know

Health and safety

⚠ Wash hands after handling bulbs and compost.

ACTIVITY 5

Life in the soil: making a wormery

Resources

- A large glass jar or tank
- Damp sand
- Damp soil
- Leaves
- Dark cloth
- Small spades/trowels
- Container for worm collection
- Watering can or container for water
- Between 10 and 20 earthworms, depending on the size of jar

Aim/concept

To introduce children to animal life underground and to show how earthworms work to improve the quality of our soil so that our plants grow well.

Process

- Prior to the activity, select a good sized patch of soil and water well, explaining that this will encourage the worms to the surface to breathe. (They may otherwise drown in the water-logged soil.)
- Using the trowels/spades, ask the children to gently dig over the patch of soil and carefully collect several worms.
- Talk about their size, how they like the dark and what they like to eat.
- Encourage the children to put alternate layers of damp soil and sand into the jar/tank, finally finishing with the worms and the leaves.
- Cover completely with a dark cloth.
- After a few days, remove the cloth. The children will see how the worms have moved, made tunnels and mixed up the layers.
- Continue to encourage them to study how the worms burrow, letting water and air move through the soil, which is great news for plant roots!
- Release the worms carefully back into the garden once the children have lost their interest.

Vocabulary/discussion

- Discuss the difference in worm size.
- How many were collected?
- Talk about how they move and how they feed. (They squeeze their muscles and have bristles on their bodies to grip the soil.) They are quite strong; birds sometimes find it difficult to pull them out of the ground.
- Discuss how they swallow soil and feed on rotting parts of dead plants and leaves, which they then pass out of their bodies. This often contains minerals which are good for the roots of our growing flowers and vegetables.

Group size

4–6

Extension ideas

1. Link the activity to a theme on planting and growing or underground insect/animal life.
2. Encourage children to observe and draw what's happening in the wormery.
3. Provide child-friendly reference books for further investigation.

Links to Foundation Stage Curriculum

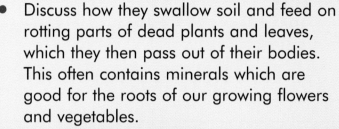

PSE	Show care and concern for others, for living things and the environment (SS)
ELG	Understand what is right, what is wrong, and why
MD	Use size language such as 'big' and 'little' (SS)
ELG	Use language such as 'circle' or 'bigger' to describe the shape and size of solids and flat shapes
KUW	Examine objects and living things to find out more about them (SS)
ELG	Find out about, and identify, some features of living things, objects and events they observe

Health and safety

⚠ Wash hands after handling the soil and worms.

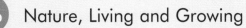

ACTIVITY
6 Pumpkin playtime

Resources

- Medium-sized pumpkin
- Sharp knife
- Spoons, colander, access to tap water
- Container for holding the pulp and seeds
- Large threading needles and strong cotton
- Shallow baking tin, access to oven, tea towel/cloth
- Night light

Aim/concept

To encourage children to see that a pumpkin is a natural and versatile resource, offering original and fun opportunities for creative play.

Process

Lantern

- With the children, look at the pumpkin and talk about its shape, colour and uses e.g. making a lantern for Halloween, roasting the seeds for us to eat, or raw for garden birds, or for making jewellery. Chopping up and cooking the pumpkin makes good soups and pies too.
- Use a sharp knife to cut a ring around the top of the pumpkin and remove the 'lid' (keep for later use).
- Using spoons or their hands, encourage the children to scoop out the pulp and seeds, putting them into a container, talking about what it looks, feels and smells like. Separate the seeds from the pulp by encouraging the children to rinse them in the colander, disposing of the pulp onto a compost heap if possible.
- Ensure the inside of the pumpkin is well cleaned.
- Let the children put the seeds on the cloth to drain and then place some onto a shallow baking tray and roast in a medium hot oven for approximately 5–10 mins, (Adult input needed). Allow to cool before eating.
- Sharing ideas with the children, adult to carve a friendly face on the side of the pumpkin and place a lit night-light in the base.
- To create an atmosphere, dim the lights and place the pumpkin on a heatproof surface away from children's reach, enjoying this moment of wonder in safety.

Jewellery

- Using a knotted needle threaded with double cotton, supervise the threading of the uncooked pumpkin seeds to make small pieces of jewellery, demonstrating placing the seed on the table and pushing the needle down through it as the easiest method.

Vocabulary/discussion

- Talk about the shape of the pumpkin, its size, colour and what it feels like.
- How did it grow, where did it come from?
- Is it heavy or light?
- Talk about the different ways in which the pumpkin can be used.
- Does it have a lot of seeds or just a few?

Group size

4

Extension ideas

1. Link to an activity on seasons/autumn/food.
2. Discuss in more detail how the pumpkin grew, using the seeds as the start point.
3. Save a few seeds from the pumpkin and air dry them (out of direct sunlight), place in an envelope (dated) and keep in a cool place until planting next spring.
4. Provide paint and paper/card for children to create their own pumpkin lantern pictures. Save some seeds for a collage activity.
5. The rind can be peeled from the pumpkin and the flesh chopped and cooked with some water as the basis for a soup.

Links to Foundation Stage Curriculum

CLL Respond to simple instructions (SS)

ELG Sustain attentive listening, responding to what they have heard by relevant comments, questions or actions

MD Show an awareness of similarities in shapes in the environment (SS)

ELG Use language such as 'circle' or 'bigger' to describe the shape and size of solids and flat shapes

KUW Describe simple features of objects and events (SS)

ELG Investigate objects and materials by using all of their senses as appropriate

PD Engage in activities requiring hand–eye coordination (SS)
Understand that equipment and tools have to be used safely (SS)

ELG Handle tools, objects, construction and malleable materials safely and with increasing control

CD Further explore an experience using a range of senses (SS)

ELG Express and communicate their ideas, thoughts and feelings by using a widening range of materials, suitable tools, imaginative and role play, movement, designing and making, and a variety of songs and musical instruments

Health and safety

⚠ Adult to take great care when using a sharp knife.
⚠ Explain to children that the needles are sharp and demonstrate how to use them safely.
⚠ Adult only to use the oven.
⚠ Position lit pumpkin in a safe position out of children's reach.

Introduction to winter

In winter, much of nature is closed down. The days are short with little sunshine. Hibernating animals are tucked up in their hiding places, many birds have flown to warmer climates, the trees are bare except for the evergreens, like the holly, ivy and firs. It's the time of year when everyone, including much of our wildlife, spends more time inside their homes.

However, on sunny, frosty days and wrapped up warmly, a 'wonder walk' can be a welcome break for everyone.

- The sun glistens on the frost, making the spider's web look beautiful and sparkly.
- The grass is covered in a crispy white coat.
- Paths and playgrounds can be slippery and fun to slide on.
- Winter colours can be white, icy blue, red, grey or mauve.
- Sometimes it's so cold, your nose, fingers and toes tingle.

- Regular feeding of the birds is a great way of keeping nature close to your setting. It nurtures a sense of care and responsibility in the children and, of course, is good for the birds.
- Snowy days are a real winter bonus and provide unlimited and exciting opportunities for play.
- Check the water in the bird bath or in puddles to see if it's frozen.
- Collect icicles hanging from the fence.
- Most broad-leaved trees have no leaves in winter, but they do have winter buds, for example the ash, horse chestnut (conker tree), beech and sycamore (refer back to top nature tips on pages 8–9).

Activities

7. Iceberg
8. Feeding the birds
9. Indoor bottle garden
10. Miniature wigwams
11. Christmas nature wreath
12. Modelling with beeswax

Tip. *To attract birds to your garden let a small area 'go wild', and introduce plants such as cotoneaster, grasses, groundsel, thistle, dog rose.*

ACTIVITY

7 Iceberg

Resources

- 2 balloons
- Access to a cold tap and water
- Deep freeze
- Scissors
- Water tray
- Small world provision

Aim/concept

To show, using a simple process, how extreme freezing conditions can alter the state of water and create icebergs, which can then be incorporated into children's water play.

Process

- In advance, stretch the neck of the balloon over a cold tap and fill, sharing with the children their excitement as they watch its size increase.
- Tie the end of the balloon securely and freeze.
- Ask the children how long they think it will take to freeze.
- Once frozen, cut or pull the balloon away and place iceberg in a deep water-filled tray or container.
- Encourage the children to touch and explore the iceberg.
- Ask if it is floating or sinking – or both.
- Talk about the places where icebergs are found, e.g. Arctic, North Pole. Do we have icebergs in our seas?
- Discuss how icebergs can be dangerous to ships.
- Encourage the children to access relevant small world resources and to use their ideas in creating imaginary water play. For example, whales, penguins, polar bears, boats.
- Continue to encourage and support their play and ask them to observe if there are any changes occurring to the shape/size of the iceberg.

Vocabulary/discussion

- Introduce the terms 'floating' and 'sinking', 'heavy' and 'light'.
- Name and discuss the North Pole, and the wildlife that lives there, such as polar bears and seals, or of the South Pole, penguins, and so on.
- Discuss what is happening to the iceberg during their play and why.
- Retell the story of the *Titanic* (with props if wished).

Group size

4

Extension ideas

1. Link the activity to freezing weather conditions outside, such as frozen puddles or bird bath.
2. Compare and contrast the differences in our weather conditions and animal life here to those of the Arctic. How do creatures survive there?
3. Introduce a world map or globe to highlight the distance between our two environments.
4. Talk about how ships avoid hitting icebergs today. Introduce the term 'sonar detection' (a device fitted to ships which detects underwater objects by reflected sound). Explain to the children that creatures such as dolphins and whales have an in-built sonar system which enables them to avoid hitting underwater objects such as icebergs.

Links to Foundation Stage Curriculum

PSE	Have a strong exploratory impulse (SS)
ELG	Continue to be interested, excited and motivated to learn
CLL	Use talk to connect ideas, explain what is happening and anticipate what might happen next (SS)
ELG	Use language to imagine and recreate roles and experiences
MD	Observe and use positional language (SS)
ELG	Use language such as 'greater', 'smaller', 'heavier', or 'lighter' to compare quantities
KUW	Talk about what is seen and what is happening (SS)
ELG	Look closely at similarities, differences, patterns and change
CD	Use available resources to create props to support play (SS)
SS	Play cooperatively as part of a group to act out a narrative
ELG	Use their imagination in art and design, music, dance, imaginative and role play and stories

Health and safety

⚠ Care to be taken when using scissors in cutting off the balloon.

⚠ Be aware of freezer burns. Disposable gloves could be worn if desired.

ACTIVITY

8 Feeding the birds

Resources

- A stick or bamboo pole strong enough to be securely wedged across a window
- A tree stump or log
- Bird seed
- Peanuts in their shell
- Pine cone(s)
- Pack of suet, saucepan, spoon, clear plastic bag, lollipop sticks (for use with pine cone)
- Half a coconut shell
- Breadcrumbs
- Currants
- Oats
- Bags of fruit and nuts
- An old net bag (used for holding vegetables or fruit)
- Roasted pumpkin seeds (from the pumpkin activity, page 36)
- A small upside-down bin lid placed on bricks to serve as a bird bath/water container

Aims/concepts

- To create opportunities for children to get close to nature and to 'wonder' and enjoy what they see.
- To initiate a sense of responsibility and care towards our winter bird population by providing them with a regular supply of food and water.

Process

- In advance of the activity, discuss with the children how the winter weather might affect the birds' food supply. What can they find to eat when the trees are bare and the ground is so cold and hard?
- With the children, select a suitable window or branch of a tree from which to hang the bird feed, and/or an area for the tree stump/log and water tray. In order to give the birds some protection while feeding (they are uneasy when away from cover), position the log near a bush, tree or container plant. *If cats are a problem – attract birds to places out of their reach!!*
- Demonstrate how to thread peanuts in their shells onto the wire.
- Encourage the children to fill the old net bags with a few nuts and fruit, tying securely at the top and threading wire through for hanging.
- Adult to slowly melt a pack of suet and allow to cool. Add pine cone(s). Empty bird seed into a clear plastic bag (enabling children to see what is going on), and drop the cone into the bag. Shake until well covered with seed. Remove.

- Using lollipop sticks, ask the children to make sure plenty of seed is well tucked into all the crevices of the cone.
- Attach a strong piece of string or wire securely around the base of the cone.
- Attach all feed to the pole or branch and sprinkle other food such as breadcrumbs, currants, roasted pumpkin seeds, oats, etc. on the window sill and/or tree stump. Position bird bath/water tray nearby.

Vocabulary/discussion

- Discuss how important it is now that you've started, to continue providing food and water for the birds as they very quickly come to rely on it. It is a responsibility!
- Birds will soon get used to you quietly watching from indoors – what food do they like best?
- Introduce the names of visiting birds.
- Which feeds are popular with which birds? For example, does the blue tit like the nuts or the pine cone?
- Which birds like using the hanging food and which ones like the windowsill or log?
- Have any unexpected wildlife visited the feeders? squirrels?
- Is there a difference between the male and female of a particular species, such as the blackbird?
- Discuss and organise with the children a system which will provide checks on food and water replenishment as well as keeping the areas clean.

Group size

6

Extension ideas

1. Link the activity to a wildlife survival topic.
2. Make a simple chart of the kinds of foods the birds like best.
3. Provide simple reference books for children to find their own discoveries.

Links to Foundation Stage Curriculum

CLL Know that information can be retrieved from books and computers (SS)

ELG Show an understanding of the elements of stories, such as main character, sequence of events, and openings, and how information can be found in non-fiction texts to answer questions about where, who, why and how

KUW Describe simple features of objects and events (SS)

ELG Find out about and identify some features of living things, objects and events they observe

CD Make comparisons using descriptive language (SS)

ELG Respond in a variety of ways to what they see, hear, smell, touch and feel

Health and safety

⚠ Wash hands thoroughly after contact with bird table/equipment.

ACTIVITY 9 Indoor bottle garden

Resources

- 1 large bottle or jar with a lid
- Gravel
- Damp potting compost
- A few small plants such as an African violet, fern, ivy and moss
- A thin stick, spoon and some string (tie together as a tool for lifting plants into position and pressing the soil in and around them)
- Water and child-size watering can

Aim/concept

To show how clever plants are: by recycling the water taken up in their roots and given off through their leaves, they can grow well and survive without the need for watering.

Process

- Place the bottle or jar on its side, explaining that the plants are to be placed inside.
- Talk about the names of the plants, asking the children what they might need to help them grow.
- Encourage them to consider how they might get the gravel, soil and plants inside. (Leave the spoon and stick untied initially.)
- Spoon into the bottle a layer of gravel followed by the damp potting compost.
- Water the plants well before gently pressing down into the moist soil with the back of the spoon.
- Put the lid on the bottle and place in a warm, shady–light position. The plants should continue to grow well without further watering.

Vocabulary/discussion

- Names of chosen plants – ivy, African violet, fern and moss.
- Discuss how the bottle garden works. The plants get water through their roots and lose it through their leaves. It is then trapped inside the bottle and trickles down for them to use again and again.

Group size

4

Extension ideas

1. Link the activity to an environmental topic, such as The Elements (water, fire, earth, air).
2. Discuss how the water being used over and over again in the bottle garden is the same process by which the earth also recycles its water:
   - Water falls from the sky and collects in lakes, rivers, reservoirs and seas.
   - The sun heats some of the water and turns it into an invisible gas called water vapour which rises in the air.
   - Some of the water vapour evaporates or disappears, but some rises and cools and turns back into liquid water, forming rain clouds.
   - Explain that it is a never-ending journey called the 'water cycle'.

Links to Foundation Stage Curriculum

PSE Display high levels of involvement in activities (SS)

ELG Continue to be interested, excited and motivated to learn

CLL Question why things happen and give explanations (SS)

ELG Sustain attentive listening, responding to what they have heard by relevant comments, questions or actions

MD Count up to three or four objects by saying one number name for each item (SS)

ELG Use developing mathematical ideas and methods to solve practical problems

KUW Show an interest in why things happen and how things work (SS)

ELG Ask questions about why things happen and how things work

PD Engage in activities requiring hand–eye coordination (SS)

SS Use one-handed tools and equipment

ELG Handle tools, objects, construction and malleable materials safely and with increasing control

Health and safety

⚠ No items to be put in mouths.
⚠ Hands to be washed well after the activity.

10 Miniature wigwams

Resources

For each wigwam:

- 5 small, evenly sized sticks, approx. 35 cm high
- Strong garden twine
- Selection of natural items to weave in and around the stick, e.g. small evergreen branches such as conifer, spruce, cypress, ivy (without berries), leaves, strips of fake fur, strands of straw, thin bendy twigs such as willow
- Strips of different coloured raffia
- Moss
- Scissors
- Pieces of card on which to stand the completed wigwams

Aim/concept

To show how to construct wigwams using natural resources.

Process

- Ask the children to select 5 sticks and, with adult help, interlink them near the top and tie securely, spreading outwards towards the base to create the wigwam shape. Leave an opening on one side for the entrance.
- Explain and discuss the range of natural resources available for them to use, and talk about the kinds of materials the native Americans would have used.
- Encourage them to select their choice using the twine and/or raffia to form the main structure.
- Secure at the base of the stick at one side of the entrance, and help them to weave in and out around the wigwam until the other side of the entrance is reached, and again tie securely.
- Supervise the children as they continue up and around the wigwam, creating their own individual designs and weaving twigs, branches, leaves, etc. into any remaining spaces or gaps.
- Complete by placing the wigwam on a board if wished and laying moss or leaves inside to create a soft base.

Vocabulary/discussion

- Names of chosen materials, e.g. evergreens such as cypress, spruce, ivy.
- Using reference books, discuss where native Americans lived and how they would make their wigwams using natural resources available to them in and around their area, from forests and mountains.
- Explain that the fur would not have been fake: they would have used deer skins and buffalo hides.
- Share ideas on family life within the wigwam. How big do you think they may have made them? How many people would live inside? How would they keep

Group size

4

Extension ideas

1. Discuss in greater detail the native American way of life, including the different names of tribes, e.g. Sioux, Apache, etc.
2. Further explore the size, shape and construction of real wigwams, providing access to child-friendly resource books.
3. Display the wigwams in a suitable area which allows for further discussion and extension of their ideas, for example introducing small world provision such as animals and people, to create an Apache camp, or any other role play scenario the children may wish to follow.
4. Suggest that they may like to access small junk modelling provision to make further props, such as fires or trees.
5. Link to a theme on different cultures and/or 'How other people lived'.
6. Read *The Garden* by Dyan Sheldon and Gary Blythe (Hutchinson Children's Books). A magical story about an American Indian Brave visiting a child in her dream.

Links to Foundation Stage Curriculum

PSE	Persist for extended periods of time at an activity of their choosing (SS)
ELG	Maintain attention, concentrate, and sit quietly when appropriate
CLL	Talk activities through, reflecting on and modifying what they are doing (SS)
ELG	Use language to imagine and recreate roles and experiences
MD	Sustain interest for a length of time on a pre-decided construction or arrangement (SS)
ELG	Use everyday words to describe position
KUW	Join construction pieces together to build and balance (SS)
ELG	Build and construct with a wide range of objects, selecting appropriate resources, and adapting their work where necessary

Health and safety

⚠ Be aware of sharp edges on sticks etc.

ACTIVITY 11 Christmas nature wreath

Resources

A selection from the following:

- Acorns/acorn shells, teasels, pine cones
- Hawthorn berries (haws), wild rose hips
- Dogwood (shiny black berries)
- Spindle berries (pretty pink berries)
- Holly and berries, Ivy, dried leaves, pine needles (spruce)
- Ash seeds, old man's beard
- Hazel nuts and walnut shells
- Herbs, e.g. rosemary and thyme, and cinnamon sticks

Plus:

- PVA glue, large bristle paintbrushes, table covering
- Large and small circular plate or bowl, large piece of heavy duty cardboard (A2)
- Sharp blade, e.g. Stanley knife (to be used by adult only on a hard, protected surface)
- Christmas CD (optional) as a focus for sharing past experience

Aim/concept

To provide the opportunity for outdoor winter investigation with a purpose – to look for and collect natural objects suitable for a nature wreath to celebrate Christmas.

Process

In advance, explain to the children that natural resources to make the wreaths will need to be collected from home, or on a 'wonder walk'.

- Draw a ring using a large plate and a bowl as your template.
- Cut out the ring using a sharp blade (on a hard, protected surface).
- Make two holes about 5 cm apart and 2.5 cm from the outside edge for the hanging ribbon.
- Show the children the cut-out rings, and explore and discuss the collected natural resources together.
- Encourage the children to use their senses in investigating the shape, smell, colour and texture of the resources they choose.
- Provide generous amounts of PVA glue to help children secure their resources, covering the wreath completely. Admire their work.
- Allow the wreath to dry (overnight or longer). The glue will dry to an attractive shiny gloss, especially on the nuts and berries. Hang on ribbon.

Vocabulary/ discussion

- Names of chosen flora, e.g. acorn (oak), holly berries, ash seeds, etc.
- Introduce and discuss the terms 'deciduous' and 'evergreen'.
- Emphasise the importance of not eating wild berries – great for wildlife but not always for us.
- Discuss and reflect upon the celebration of Christmas and create an awareness of cultural and religious differences.

Group size

4

Extension ideas

1. Discuss animal hibernation and survival through the winter months.
2. Link the activity to a topic/theme on wildlife.
3. Discuss and explain in more detail the terms 'deciduous' and 'evergreen' with examples. Why do trees lose their leaves?

Links to Foundation Stage Curriculum

PSE Make connections between different parts of their life experience (SS)

ELG Understand that people have different needs, views, cultures and beliefs, that need to be treated with respect

MD Show an interest in shape and space by playing with shapes or making arrangements with objects (SS)

ELG Use everyday words to describe position

KUW Examine objects and living things to find out more about them (SS)

ELG Investigate objects and materials by using all of their senses as appropriate

PD Manipulate materials to achieve a planned effect (SS)

ELG Handle tools, objects, construction and malleable materials safely and with increasing control

CD Begin to describe the texture of things (SS)

ELG Explore colour, texture, shape, form and space in two or three dimensions

Show an interest in what they see, hear, smell, touch and feel (SS)

ELG Respond in a variety of ways to what they see, hear, smell, touch and feel

Health and safety

⚠ Be aware of poisonous berries.
⚠ Children must not put items in their mouths.

ACTIVITY 12 Modelling with beeswax

Resources

- A selection of modelling beeswax cut into small pieces. (It is best to offer just one or two colours initially
  a) to reduce colour competition among the group, and
  b) to keep the individual colours pure.)
- A small supply of simple resources. For example, thin pieces of wire, pebbles or small twigs can support creativity and the stability of models
- A bag or box for storing the beeswax

Aim/concept

To introduce children to a delightful and truly natural reusable modelling material.

Process

- If it is a very cold day, prior to the activity, place the pieces of beeswax on a baking tray near (not on) a heat source to warm slightly.
- Ask the children to choose a piece of beeswax from the selection and to warm it in their hands.
- Using their fingers, encourage them to manipulate the beeswax by kneading, pushing, pulling, twisting, rubbing and carefully stretching it out until it almost becomes transparent.

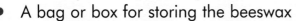

- Explore the product with the children, encouraging them to use their sense of touch and smell.
- Briefly explain that bees make wax to build their combs to store their honey (honeycomb), and that after the honey is extracted in late August/early September, the remaining wax is the bee's second most useful product of the hive and can be used for making candles and furniture polish.
- Talk about bees. Why don't we see them in winter time?
- Continue to supervise them in their exploration of the beeswax, working it and flexing it into shapes and models if they so wish, using the resources to support their creations.
- Gradually introduce other colours, if desired.

Vocabulary/discussion

- Discuss how the beeswax feels and smells.
- Explain that bees are 'wintered down' in their hives from autumn onwards, and if their honey has been removed for us to eat, the beekeeper must replace their food source by feeding them with a sugar syrup, to help them survive throughout the winter months.
- Explain that the warm days of spring draw them out of their hives in search of pollen- and nectar-giving plants and trees, enabling them once again to begin the honey-making process.
- Talk about wax crayons. How similar or different are they?

Group size

4–6

Extension ideas

1. Link the activity to a winter hibernation topic.
2. Discuss further the life of the bee and its value and importance in our natural world.
3. Help the children decorate white (shop bought) candles by warming tiny pieces of thin coloured wax in their hands and pressing firmly to make a design of their choice.

Links to Foundation Stage Curriculum

PSE	Show curiosity (SS)
ELG	Continue to be interested, excited and motivated to learn
CLL	Talk activities through, reflecting on and modifying what they are doing (SS)
ELG	Use talk to organise, sequence and clarify thinking, ideas, feelings and events
KUW	Investigate construction materials (SS)
ELG	Select the tools and techniques they need to shape, assemble and join materials they are using
PD	Explore malleable materials by patting, stroking, poking, squeezing, pinching and twisting them (SS)
	Manipulate materials to achieve a planned effect (SS)
ELG	Handle tools, objects, construction and malleable materials safely and with increasing control
CD	Work creatively on a large or small scale (SS)
ELG	Explore colour, texture, shape, form and space in two or three dimensions

Health and safety

⚠ Do not place the product on a direct heat source.

Introduction to spring

Spring is the season of rebirth – after many months of resting, nature begins to wake up, and with each warm day, our natural world gradually comes to life. As the days lengthen and the sun gets warmer, the children will welcome the opportunity for a spring 'wonder walk'. It is nature's busiest time of year, and after such a long sleep, a whole lot of activity will be taking place.

- After the ice-cold colours of winter, spring brings shades of green, yellow, pale blues and pinks.

- Birds become very active, looking for a mate to prepare for nesting. The spot they choose is very special and important to them, as they will raise their babies there. Can the children recognise any of the species. What colour are they? You may also see them carrying bits of grass, feathers, small pieces of moss in their beaks. This is what they are collecting to make their nest. If you see them carrying a worm, they may well be feeding their young. Children need to watch nest activity standing well back, otherwise the parent will become anxious and abandon it, possibly leaving the babies to starve.

- Hedgehogs, badgers, dormice and some insects, such as bees and ladybirds, begin to emerge from hibernation.

- Flowers such as daffodils, crocuses, tulips, snowdrops and, later on, bluebells, are beginning to open up their petals; just in time for early visiting bees to feed on the sugary nectar inside. Any bulbs planted by the children in autumn (see Activity 4, page 32), should now be budding and flowering.

- Broad-leaved trees will also be unfurling their bright green new leaves and flowers. Look out for pussy willows and catkins (hazel tree). Some, like the flowering cherry, will be getting ready to burst open with pink blossom – again, just in time for the insects to feed from them.

- Look in ponds in March and April for frogspawn.
- Make a tadpole aquarium. See page 58.
- Farmers will be busy preparing the sheep for their new lambs to be born.
- Ducks will be sitting on their riverside nests, waiting for their eggs to hatch.

Activities

13. Streamer crowns, streamer sticks
14. Springtime saucer gardens
15. Tadpole aquarium
16. Growing and planting beans (link to summer activities: 'Bean tepee', page 68, 'Summer potato and 'bean harvest', page 78)
17. Easy grow potatoes (link to 'Summer potato and bean harvest', page 78)
18. Leaf tiles

ACTIVITY 13 Streamer crowns, streamer sticks

Resources

- For crowns – one piece of thin cane to fit child's head. Strengthen by holding both ends together and twisting so that it wraps around itself
- For sticks – cut sticks, dowel or cane to about 30 cm in length
- Strong clear tape
- For streamers – a selection of coloured crepe paper and/or ribbons about 60 cm long
- String and a pen for measuring

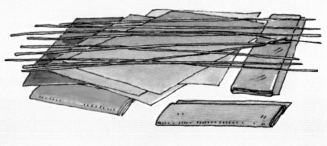

Aim/concept

To allow for creative and easy investigation of the wind on the first few warm days of spring.

Process

- Ask the children if they would like to make a streamer crown or stick, and to select the appropriate resource.

Crowns

- Using the string as a rule, encourage the children to measure around each other's heads and to then mark the correct length on the cane.
- Assist the children in twisting, then bending it to fit around their head.
- Help them secure the ends with tape.
- Attach their chosen streamers (about 4–7) to the crown by folding one end over and taping it both to itself and to the cane.

Sticks

- Twist their chosen streamers tightly together at one end and using the tape, attach securely to one end of the stick.
- Talk about the weather outside – is it nice and windy?
- Using the streamers outside, encourage the children to 'catch the wind'. (The crowns can also be held high above the head.)

Vocabulary/discussion

- Encourage the children to share ideas and observations on how they know spring has arrived.
- Name the different colours and count the number of streamers chosen.
- Discuss with the children what they may need to think about to be safe, when running and playing outside with their streamers.

Group size

4–6

Extension ideas

1. Link the activity to a theme or topic on the weather or the power of the wind.
2. Encourage the children to use a tape and state the measurement before marking it off on the cane.
3. Discuss the differences and similarities in head size.
4. When outside, ask the children to observe from which direction the wind is blowing.
5. Consider possibly introducing a compass and/or making a weather vane to find out wind direction.
6. Explore in more detail the first signs of spring and read *When Will It Be Spring*? by Catherine Walters (Magi Publications).

Links to Foundation Stage Curriculum

PSE Have an awareness of the boundaries set and behavioural expectations within the setting (SS)

ELG Consider the consequences of their words and actions for themselves and others

MD Use mathematical language in play (SS)

ELG Use developing mathematical ideas and methods to solve practical problems

PD Negotiate an appropriate pathway when walking, running or using a wheelchair or other mobility aids both indoors and outdoors (SS)

ELG Show awareness of space, of themselves and of others

Health and safety

⚠ Streamers not to be used indoors.
⚠ No bumping into or poking others with the sticks.
⚠ Adults to ensure adequate space is available for children to run safely.

ACTIVITY 14 # Springtime saucer gardens

Resources

- Small clay saucers/dishes – about 10–15 cm diameter, purchased, made previously, or donated from home
- A small bag of potting compost
- A water mister (plastic spray bottle)
- Large spoons
- A small amount of quick growing grass seed, or moss if an instant garden is required
- Scissors for shaping moss (and cutting grass once it has grown)
- Selection of natural props, e.g. catkin and/or forsythia twigs, cherry blossom, pussy willow, small shells or half walnuts for 'ponds', twigs and gravel or small stones)
- Small pieces of tissue for use as small balls of blossom to be attached to bare twigs

Aim/concept

To provide an opportunity for individual creative and imaginary investigation of nature, by bringing a little piece of springtime inside.

Process

- Discuss with the children their observations of what is happening outside at this time of year.
- Explain that in the dishes you have provided, they can create their own springtime garden.
- Using the spoons (or their hands if they'd prefer) let them fill their dishes three-quarters full.
- Demonstrate how to moisten the soil well using the water spray.

If using grass seed:
- Help the children sprinkle enough seed to cover the surface well (but not too thickly).
- Help them to gently cover this with a thin layer of compost.
- Ask the children to carefully position an upside-down shell or walnut half for their pond.
- Let them add catkins, twigs, etc.

If using moss:

- Children will need to moisten the soil well before positioning their 'pond'. They then need to carefully press and shape the moss firmly in and around their pond, taking it to the edge of the dish.
- Place the gardens on a warm sunny windowsill and spray with water every day (this gentle action will not dislodge the seeds). Wait for the grass to grow.
- Once the grass seed has sprouted, encourage the children to touch, feel and observe the natural resources, supporting them in their care for their gardens.
- Continued water spraying of the gardens will prolong their 'shelf' life.

Vocabulary/discussion

- Name the natural resources, e.g. forsythia, pussy willow, catkins, cherry blossom, etc.
- Discuss in detail the changes taking place outside. How do the children know it is springtime?

Group size

4–6

Extension ideas

1. Link the activity to a theme or topic on 'How plants grow' or 'The seasons'.
2. Encourage creative play and use of language by suggesting they may like to build up a seasonal story when constructing their gardens.
3. Use modelling beeswax (see winter activity, page 50) to create additional small props such as insects, birds, nests or animals.

Links to Foundation Stage Curriculum

PSE Demonstrate a sense of pride in own achievement (SS)

ELG Select and use activities and resources independently

KUW Show an interest in the world in which they live (SS)

ELG Observe, find out about and identify features in the place they live and the natural world

CD Work creatively on a large or small scale (SS)

ELG Explore colour, texture, shape, form and space in two or three dimensions

Health and safety

⚠ Ensure hands are washed after handling soil and plants.

ACTIVITY

15 Tadpole aquarium

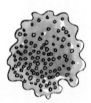

Resources

- A good sized glass or plastic tank or aquarium
- Water – preferably collected in a water butt or from the pond is best. If not possible, leave tap water to stand for 24 hours, to allow any anti-bacterial chemicals to evaporate
- A small amount of frogspawn (collected from ponds in a jar) and/or tadpoles
- Fresh pond plants for supplying oxygen and food for the newly hatched tadpoles
- A stone, large enough to protrude from the water
- Mud from the sides or bottom of the pond, or clean sand and gravel
- Netting or grid to cover top of tank
- One or two great pond snails, which will eat the algae and help keep the water clear

Aim/concept

To study the life cycle of the frog and to encourage children to reflect and consider the fact that when first born, the tadpole does not resemble its parents at all, neither does it depend upon them for survival, unlike many other species, including ourselves, which do.

Process

- Place the aquarium in a safe, light position, but not in direct sunlight.
- Explain to the children the importance of using pond (or 'stood') water.
- Gently empty the frogspawn or tadpoles into the tank.
- Explain to the children what will be needed, such as light, pond-weed, etc.
- Around 10 days after the spawn has been laid, the little tadpoles emerge, and as they have no mouths at first, live on the remains of the yolk. Encourage the children to check each day for any signs of this.
- After a day or two, their mouths develop and they will start to nibble the water plants provided. Watch them with the children.
- Encourage the children to study the tadpoles, using magnifying glasses if necessary, and to be aware of when the water becomes cloudy and smells unpleasant – it's time to change the water! Talk through the process for this with the children.
- Ask the children to make sure there is always a supply of fresh pond-weed.
- After approximately two weeks, the tadpoles will also need to be fed raw meat (in their natural habitat, they would be starting to eat tiny pond

insects). Tie tiny morsels with thread, hanging them from the netting or grid cover. Replace with a fresh supply every two days.

- Talk about the changes taking place to the tadpoles over the following weeks.
- Continue to provide a safe and healthy environment for the froglets to thrive.
- At approximately 10–12 weeks, they will want to climb onto the stone to gulp air into their new lungs – it is therefore time to return them to the pond! Ask the children why this is necessary.

Vocabulary/discussion

- Name the features of the tadpole at various stages of development, e.g. frogspawn, gills for breathing, back legs, tails, etc.
- Talk about what the tadpoles need to help them grow, e.g. oxygen, food, clean water.
- Discuss with the children and encourage them to think about the differences between the life cycle of the frog and other animal babies, which, unlike the tadpole, may look like their mum and dad and need them to help them survive.

Group size

4–6

Extension ideas

1. Link to a theme or topic on families.
2. Link to a theme on life cycles/seasons.
3. Organise with the children a system of feeding and water replenishment.
4. Encourage children to keep a diary of observed changes.
5. Provide simple reference books for enjoyment and confirmation of the cycle.
6. If possible, photograph the pond where the froglets are released as a memory for the children.

Links to Foundation Stage Curriculum

PSE	Show care and concern for others, living things and the environment (SS)
ELG	Understand what is right, what is wrong, and why
CLL	Use talk to connect ideas, explain what is happening and anticipate what might happen next (SS)
ELG	Use talk to organise, sequence and clarify thinking, ideas, feelings and events
KUW	Begin to differentiate between past and present, e.g. life cycles of plants/animals (SS)
ELG	Find out about past and present events in their own lives, and in those of their families and other people they know

Health and safety

⚠ Aquarium items not to be put in the mouth.
⚠ Hands always washed after involvement in the activity.

ACTIVITY 16 Growing and planting beans

Resources

For growing

- A jar for each child
- Paper towels
- Handful of beans: runner or a French climbing variety are ideal
- Water

For planting

- A plastic flowerpot and saucer for each child
- Potting compost
- Water
- Canes or sticks for support

Aim/concept

- For children to observe how seeds grow and to show that well-cared-for bean plants will provide healthy food to eat.

Process

- Encourage the children to explore the bean. Is it hard? Can they break it? Soaking a bean in water overnight will soften it so it can be split open to see what's inside. In one half they will see a very tiny baby plant ready to grow and in the other, its food store.
- Ask them to think about what the bean seeds might need to help them grow.
- Line the jars with paper towels and add a little water, supporting the children in placing two beans on different sides, halfway up each jar and next to the glass.
- Keep the paper towels moist and keep the beans indoors. After a few days ask the children what changes they can see.
- Explain that the beans have germinated. They have sprouted shoots which grow towards the light, and roots which grow down towards the ground and water. They are now ready to start growing.
- Plant the beans and encourage the children to observe changes e.g. how many leaves has the shoot grown? What has happened to the seed case? Are there more roots? How many?
- Once the seedling looks tall and healthy with plenty of leaves and roots, it is time to transplant it to its own individual pot.

- Using damp potting compost, ask the children to each fill a flowerpot, making a hole in the centre deep enough for the seedling's roots. Stand the pot in a saucer.
- Very carefully (the stem is very delicate), remove the paper towel from the jar and plant one seedling in each pot, pressing compost firmly in and around each one to keep it upright. Tying a plant carefully to a stick or cane will help it to grow straight.
- Place in a warm, sunny position and water regularly (about every three days).

Vocabulary/discussion

- Name parts of the plant and its growing process: seed, shoots, roots, seedlings, germination, and so on.
- Discuss other kinds of seeds e.g. pips in an apple, pine cone seeds, cherry stone, etc.
- Talk about what plants need to help them grow and how some grow very quickly, while others can take many years.

Group size

4–6

Extension ideas

1. Link to making a bean tepee on page 68.
2. Compare plants grown in different conditions: sun, dark, regular/non-regular water, and so on.
3. Place a carnation or celery stick in water containing blue ink or food colouring. What happens?
4. Measure and record height of plants.
5. Read books such as *Jack and the Beanstalk*, traditional.

Links to Foundation Stage Curriculum

PSE Show curiosity (SS)
ELG Continue to be interested, excited and motivated to learn
MD Observe and use positional language (SS)
ELG Use language such as 'greater', 'smaller', 'heavier', or 'lighter', to compare quantities
KUW Examine objects and living things to find out more about them (SS)
ELG Find out about, and identify, some features of living things, objects and events they observe

Health and safety

⚠ Children to wash hands after handling compost.

ACTIVITY
17 Easy grow potatoes

Resources

- One early variety seed potato, to plant late March/April
- An old tyre, two if possible
- A good, rich growing compost
- A scoop and/or small spades

Aim/concept

To demonstrate how simple it is to grow our own food and that one seed potato can provide enough new potatoes for several 'small' people to enjoy!

Process

- Examine the seed potato with the children, counting the protruding sprouts but being careful not to knock them off.
- Explain that it is from these sprouts (should be between two and four per potato) that the potato plant will grow.
- Place one tyre on the ground outside in a sunny position. Using garden tools or their hands, encourage the children to fill the tyre with the compost.
- In the centre, let them make a planting hole of approximately 10–15 cm deep, placing the seed potato within it with the little sprouts facing upwards.
- Cover carefully with more compost and water well.
- Water weekly or every few days depending on the weather conditions.
- When the plant is approximately 10 cm tall, ask the children to help you carefully place another tyre on the top and fill again with the compost. The plant will also grow up through the soil in this tyre and develop flowers.
- Continue watering throughout the growing period – do not let the compost become dry. Encourage the children to take turns at this.
- The crop is ready after the flowers have died back and the leaves may be turning yellow (from July onwards).
- Refer to Activity 24 on page 78 for harvesting activity.

Vocabulary/discussion

- Name the potato variety and talk about the time of year it was planted and the season in which the crop will be ready.
- Discuss the many uses of potato in our everyday diet. For example, where do chips come from?
- Talk about how the children might use their crop of potatoes when they are ready – introduce the terms 'raw' and 'cooked'.

Group size

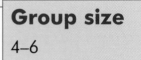

4–6

Extension ideas

1. Link the activity to a theme or topic on food.
2. Discuss similarities and differences in the size of potatoes (provide a selection).
3. Discuss in more detail the food value of the potatoes and different cooking methods/recipes.
4. Weigh some potatoes.
5. Using one tyre only, apply the same growing method in order to produce a pumpkin (this will be ready to harvest in autumn).
6. Read *Oliver's Vegetables* by Vivian French (Hodder Children's Books).

Links to Foundation Stage Curriculum

CLL	Extend vocabulary, especially by grouping and naming (SS)
ELG	Extend their vocabulary, exploring the meanings and sounds of new words
MD	Count up to three or four objects by saying one number name for each item (SS)
ELG	Count reliably up to 10 everyday objects
KUW	Show an awareness of change (SS)
ELG	Look closely at similarities, differences, patterns and change
PD	Show awareness of own needs with regard to eating, sleeping and hygiene (SS)
ELG	Recognise the importance of keeping healthy and those things which contribute to this

Health and safety

- ⚠ Children must not pick or eat the flowers or leaves from the plant.
- ⚠ Hands to be washed after handling soil and plant.

18 Leaf tiles

Resources

- 2 cups of plain flour
- 1 cup of salt
- 1 cup of water
- 2 tablespoons of cooking oil
- A large mixing bowl and spoon
- Flour for rolling
- Rolling pins and boards
- A variety of leaves from the broad-leaved group, such as oak, ash, beech, horse chestnut, fruit trees, etc., and some from the conifer group, e.g. spruce, scots pine, larch and fir
- Paint or varnish

Aim/concept

To increase the children's awareness of the arrival of spring by identifying a range of leaves and collecting new leaves for creating a leaf tile.

Process

In advance of the activity collect leaves from outdoors with the children.
- Explore and discuss the collected leaves, looking at the difference in their shape, size and colour.
- Talk about the trees they may have come from and ask the children to set aside their choice of leaf for their tile.
- Supervise the children as they measure out the 'clay' ingredients into the mixing bowl, helping them to mix it well with the spoon.
- Ask them to scatter a little flour onto their boards to keep the clay from sticking.
- With the help of the children's assessment, adult to divide the mixture equally between the group.
- Encourage them to use their hands to knead the clay into a ball.
- Using a floured rolling pin, help them roll it flat to about 3 cm thickness, making sure the tile size matches that of the leaf chosen by each child.
- Again using the rolling pin, support them in pressing the leaf, vein side down, onto the tile so that it leaves a print, then help them carefully remove it.
- Adult to bake the tiles for about 2 hours at 150°C (300°F), Gas mark 2.
- Once cooled, encourage the children to paint or varnish their tiles.

Vocabulary/discussion

- Name the chosen leaves and talk about the trees in and around their environment, from which they came.
- Name the two groups of trees – broad-leaved and conifer – and share observations on the differences in shape, size and texture.
- Ask the children to think about which group of trees lose their leaves in winter.
- Discuss how trees sprout from a seed, grow tall and produce flowers and fruits, but take many, many years to do so.

Group size

4

Extension ideas

1. Introduce the terms and meaning of the words evergreen and deciduous. (Most broad-leaved trees are deciduous, while most conifers are evergreen.)
2. Talk about how leaves in spring compare to leaves in autumn.
3. Provide magnifying glasses for closer study of the leaf.
4. Provide reference books for enjoyment and identification of trees.
5. Discuss the importance and value of trees within our environment.
6. Supply paint for tile painting.
7. Provide access to small mixing pots and green and white paint only, to allow for individual colour-matching of leaves.
8. Provide labels giving leaf tiles their tree names.
9. Read *The Secret Life of Trees* by Chiara Chevallier (DK Eyewitness Readers, Level 2).

Links to Foundation Stage Curriculum

PSE	Demonstrate a sense of pride in own achievement (SS)
ELG	Select and use activities and resources independently
MD	Use size language such as 'big' and 'little' (SS)
ELG	Use language such as 'circle' or 'bigger' to describe the shape and size of solids and flat shapes
KUW	Show an interest in the world in which they live (SS)
ELG	Observe, find out about and identify features in the place they live and the natural world
PD	Manipulate materials to achieve a planned effect (SS)
ELG	Handle tools, objects, construction and malleable materials safely and with increasing control
CD	Make constructions, collages, paintings, drawings and dances (SS)
ELG	Explore colour, texture, shape, form and space in two or three dimensions

Introduction to summer

Summertime entices us outside, tempting us with its warm sunshine, longer days and blue skies. We are presented with an abundance of opportunities for outdoor pleasure, the lushness of nature is free for all to see and explore. It's the time of year when nature can proudly exhibit and celebrate its achievements and all its hard work throughout the year. Colours are strong and powerful: yellows, greens, blues and reds are reflected in an abundance of flowers, trees, butterflies, insects, fruits and vegetables. A summer 'wonder walk' can lead to a picnic under shady trees, where the children can lie down and look up

through the branches and watch the leaves move and rustle in the breeze, and consider what animal, bird and insect life exists within it.

The links between the seasons will begin to make sense to the children; they can see the rewards and benefit of their spring planting and creating of wild patches in their outdoor environment. Summertime will 'bring it all to life'.

- Summer vegetable harvest – picking and eating beans, peas, potatoes and tomatoes.
- Summer fruit harvest – strawberries, redcurrants, blackcurrants and raspberries.
- Outside dens can easily and spontaneously be erected from sheets and cloths.
- Sand and water play equipment can be taken outside. Extend play

opportunities by adding stones, moss, logs, pebbles, shells, etc. to make a 'lake', 'pond', 'beach' or 'island'.

- Daisy and dandelion chains can be made, creating necklaces or crowns.

- An abundance of insect activity exists for children to observe, such as grasshoppers, beetles, dragonflies, bees, ladybirds, moths and butterflies.

- Look out for caterpillars on stinging nettles, leaves and grasses. If you see some, carefully remove with the plant it was found on and place in a large tank out of direct sunlight. Continue to feed the caterpillars with a fresh supply of the same leaf/grass. The children may be lucky enough to see the caterpillar turn into a pupa, where the adult moth or butterfly will be growing inside. It will be one of nature's great 'wonders' for them to see it emerge as a butterfly (or moth) later on in the summer. When this happens, gently release it back into its natural habitat.

Activities

19. Bean tepee (links to the 'Growing and planting beans' activity, page 60, and 'Summer potato and bean harvest', page 78)

20. Observing mini-beast habitats and creating an indoor zoo

21. Rosa's treasure game

22. Summer scented flower containers

23. Scented flower pouches

24. Summer potato and bean harvest (links to the 'Growing and planting beans' activity, page 60, 'Easy grow potatoes', page 62, and 'Bean tepee' activity, page 68).

ACTIVITY
19 Bean tepee

Resources

- A suitable outdoor space
- Spades and trowels
- Five or six sticks, branches or bamboo poles, min. length 5ft
- Strong garden twine
- About 10–12 bean plants, available from garden centres or farmers' markets, or left over from Activity 16 on page 60.
- Watering can
- A small amount of rich compost to dig into soil

Aim/concept

To provide a special 'living den' for outdoor play which will also give a fresh supply of good food.

Process

- Prior to activity (late April), place the bean plants outside in a sheltered area in order to acclimatise them to outdoor weather conditions.
- Explore the garden with the children to locate a suitable position for planting – a sunny spot is best.
- Using spades and trowels, clear a circle of ground, about 4ft in diameter, removing any grass, weeds or large stones, etc. Dig in some good compost to enrich the soil.
- Discuss with the children where the opening will be for the entrance.
- Supervise them as they position the sticks/poles around the outer edge of the circle. (Adult input will be needed to assist in pushing the stakes into the ground.)
- Adult to firmly secure the interlocking tops (tepee style), using strong twine.
- Ask the children to plant the beans in holes of about 15 cm deep and 15 cm apart around the outside of each stake. Two or three plants should ensure a good bushy growth.
- Press the soil firmly down in and around each plant and water well.
- Secure any tendrils from the plant as they grow up and around the stakes. The tepee den will become more private as the plants grow upwards and outwards! To encourage side shoots and increase flowering, pinch out the growing tips when the plants have almost reached the top of their supports.
- Encourage the children to observe their growth and to watch for the flowers, the formation of the little beans, and finally picking and enjoying the cooking and tasting of this delicious vegetable. (See 'Summer potato and bean harvest', page 78.)

Don't forget to water them regularly!

Vocabulary/discussion

- Name the parts of the growing plant, e.g. tendril, flowers, baby bean, runner/French bean.
- Discuss the height of the growing plants. Is one growing faster than another?
- Share ideas and suggestions on how best to use the tepee as a special place to play, while also ensuring the plants are not damaged.
- Observe and talk about any insects or birds that visit the plants or are attracted to the flowers.
- Organise a watering rota system with the children.

Group size

4–6

Extension ideas

1. Link the activity to growing and planting beans indoors. See Activity 16, page 60.
2. Encourage the children to measure and keep a record of the height of the growing plants, the length of the beans as they grow and the number of beans picked per plant.
3. From flower to bean – discuss how long before it is ready to pick.
4. Read *Oliver's Vegetables* by Vivian French (Hodder Children's Books).

Links to Foundation Stage Curriculum

CLL Build up vocabulary that reflects their interests and experiences (SS)

ELG Extend their vocabulary, exploring the meanings and sounds of new words

MD Show awareness of symmetry (SS)

ELG Use language such as 'circle' or 'bigger' to describe the shape and size of solids and flat shapes

KUW Begin to differentiate between past and present (SS)

ELG Find out about past and present events in their own lives, and in those of their families and other people they know

PD Judge body space in relation to spaces available when fitting into confined spaces or negotiating holes and boundaries (SS)

ELG Show awareness of space, of themselves and of others

CD Work creatively on a large or small scale (SS)

ELG Explore colour, texture, shape, form and space in two or three dimensions

Health and safety

⚠ Ensure hands are washed after digging and planting.

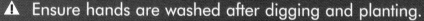

ACTIVITY 20 Observing mini-beast habitats and creating an indoor zoo

Resources

- Large glass or clear plastic container(s), with net cover
- Appropriate vegetation for mini-beasts
- Sand and/or soil for base of container
- Stones

- Small logs and/or bark
- Small screw-top jars/pots (with breathing holes), for mini-beast collection
- Magnifying glasses for observation
- Water spray bottle

Aim/concept

To encourage children to observe a variety of mini-beasts and their habitat outdoors, and to then apply that knowledge to create an indoor 'zoo'.

Process

- Choosing a suitable area outside, ask the children to place pieces of rotting wood or vegetation, bark, logs, stone, an old flowerpot placed on its side, etc., to attract small creatures.
- Over several days, encourage the children to observe the variety of mini-beasts that settle there, noting whether the mini-beasts prefer dark or light places, dry or moist. What do they eat?
- Using these observations, supervise them in creating an indoor 'zoo', replicating the appropriate habitat for each particular mini-beast.
- When collecting the mini-beasts, remind children to handle them with care, as they are very fragile. Do not collect more than you need.
- Place the container in a cool position, away from direct sunlight but not in a draught. Do not keep captive for more than a few days.
- Using the magnifying glasses, encourage the children to look at the mini-beasts every day, and to observe any changes and how they move and eat.
- Ask the children to ensure there is always a good supply of fresh food and, if necessary, to spray sparingly with water to keep moist.
- Once the study has been completed, release them carefully back into the area where they were found.

Vocabulary/discussion

- Name the various mini-beasts found.
- Name the plants on which they were found.
- Study their shapes. How many legs do they have?
- Discuss how they move, slow or fast, where do they like to hide?
- What do they feed on? Discuss the importance of the food chain.
- Introduce the term 'herbivores' (creatures that eat plants).

Group size

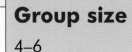

4–6

Extension ideas

1. Link the activity to a theme or topic on animal life, and life cycles.
2. Make pitfall traps by burying jam jars in a variety of habitats and bait with such things as an apple core, cheese, meat, jam.
3. Record and draw life pictures of the mini-beasts, label and display.
4. Discuss in detail how animals feed. For example, some suck the sap from inside a plant, some eat the leaf (caterpillars), and so on.
5. Provide reference books for children to continue or confirm their studies and observations.
6. Read *Bugs and Slugs* by Judy Tatchell (Usborne Lift-the-Flap Books).

Links to Foundation Stage Curriculum

PSE Have a strong exploratory impulse (SS)

ELG Be confident to try new activities, initiate ideas and speak in a familiar group

CLL Question why things happen and give explanations (SS)

ELG Sustain attentive listening, responding to what they have heard by relevant comments, questions or actions

KUW Examine objects and living things to find out more about them (SS)

ELG Find out about and identify some features of living things, objects and events they observe

Health and safety

⚠ Wash hands after handling mini-beasts and picking plants/leaves.

ACTIVITY 21 Rosa's treasure game

Resources

- Two large trays or other suitable surfaces and a cloth to cover and keep the objects from children's view
- A selection of objects, natural and man-made (about 10–12) which will be referred to in the story 'Rosa's treasure game'. Suggestions include a stone, shell, bark, cone, twig and feather, a Coke can, chocolate bar wrapper, crisp packet, a piece of (fake) fur, etc.
- Ideally the items selected for telling the story are hidden in the garden in advance

Aim/concept

To encourage children's observation and memory skills, using a mix of both natural and man-made objects, to consider which items are more easily identified when hidden in the garden.

Process

- Set a tray of objects (always relevant to the story) to the side of you, out of the children's view. Have an empty tray on your other side.
- Using the photocopiable story on page 87, talk through the story with the children, introducing each item at the appropriate time.

The story on page 87 can be adapted as required, to suit the particular age, stage and social environment relevant to the children. Names, gender and relationship between adult and child can also be subsituted.

- Encourage the children to touch and feel the objects and to participate and interact with the story, by asking them questions such as 'Where might it have come from?' or, 'How do you think it got there?'
- At the end of the story, encourage the children to recall what happened and to count and remember all the items that Rosa found. Cover the tray.
- Explain that Rosa's treasure is going to be hidden in the garden or outdoor environment and that they are going to see if they can find all the objects. (Another adult may be needed at this point to hide the 'treasure' if it has not been hidden already.)
- Encourage the children to explore their outdoor environment and to find all the 'treasure'.
- Discuss with them why some of the items were easier to find than others.

Vocabulary/discussion

- Discuss in more detail the difference between natural and man-made objects.
- Why are some items easier to see than others?
- Introduce the term 'camouflage' with examples.
- Discuss the importance of using a bin for litter or taking it home.

Group size

6

Extension ideas

1. Link to an activity on litter awareness and/or care of the environment.
2. Encourage the children to retell the story, naming the items of treasure in order.
3. Explore the term 'camouflage' with the children, explaining how animals and birds 'blend in' with their natural environment, sometimes even changing their plumage or fur colour to suit the changing seasons.
4. Provide access to appropriate reference books.
5. Provide a range of appropriate paint colours for children to make camouflage pictures.
6. Encourage children to find their own range of natural and man-made objects and to write or tell their own story.

Links to Foundation Stage Curriculum

PSE	Display high levels of involvement in activities (SS)
ELG	Maintain attention, concentrate, and sit quietly where appropriate
CLL	Listen to stories with increasing attention and recall (SS)
ELG	Sustain attentive listening, responding to what they have heard by relevant comments, questions or actions
KUW	Describe simple features of objects and events (SS)
ELG	Find out about and identify some features of living things, objects and events they observe
CD	Explore what happens when they mix colours (SS)
ELG	Explore colour, texture, shape, form and space in two or three dimensions

Health and safety

⚠ Ensure all hidden items are safe to be handled.
⚠ Children to wash hands after finding the treasure.

ACTIVITY 22 **Summer scented flower containers**

Resources

- A selection of 10–15 summer flowering plants
- Planting containers/flowerpots/tubs/old sinks, etc.
- Pebbles/stones for base to allow for water drainage
- Good growing compost
- Trowels, water and watering cans
- Labels/craft lolly sticks, pens for naming

Aim/concept

To create a sweet-smelling flower garden for children's sensory pleasure and for easy observation of summer insect visitors.

Process

- Explain to the children that they are going to create a scented flower container-garden, the smell of which will attract insects such as butterflies and bees.
- Discuss the different plants: their names, colours, size, how tall they grow and space needed. Plan planting accordingly.
- Help the children identify a suitable sunny area outside for them.
- Ensure all plants are well watered before de-potting.
- Ask the children to collect a few small (drainage) stones/pebbles to place in the base of each container.
- Using their hands or trowels, encourage them to fill the containers with compost – halfway up for large plants, higher up for smaller ones.
- Supervise them as they gently release the plant from its pot by carefully tipping it to one side, encouraging them to look at its delicate root growth.
- Place the plant into position in its container and carefully fill compost in and around the plant to the top. Press down firmly and water well.
- Remind the children that plants grown in containers need watering more than those grown in the garden. Never let the soil dry out completely, and label each pot with garden tags, sticks, and so on.

Vocabulary/discussion

- Name the plants and their parts: root, stem, leaf, bud, petal, and so on.
- Discuss shapes and perfumes of flowers as they bloom. Select favourites.
- Are bees and butterflies attracted to a particular plant or colour of plant?
- Introduce the terms 'nectar' and 'pollen'.

Group size

4–6

Extension ideas

1. Link the activity to a theme/topic on plant growth, insect life, life processes, developing sensory awareness, etc.
2. Talk about other plants that have powerful scents, such as herbs.
3. Introduce flower features: e.g. stamen (the male part), stigma (the female part), and so on.
4. Explain the importance of pollination e.g. the bee transfers pollen from flower to flower as it collects nectar. This helps the flower to make new seeds.
5. Allow some flower heads to develop seeds to show the children how the process works.

Links to Foundation Stage Curriculum

PSE	Have a strong exploratory impulse (SS)
ELG	Continue to be interested, excited and motivated to learn
CLL	Know that information can be retrieved from books and computers (SS)
KUW	Examine objects and living things to find out more about them (SS)
ELG	Find out about, and identify, some features of living things, objects and events they observe

Health and safety

⚠ Wash hands after handling compost and plants.
⚠ Only craft lolly sticks to be used, not from collected sources.

ACTIVITY 23

Scented flower pouches

Resources

- A selection of flower heads, such as honeysuckle, clematis, lavender, cow parsley, stocks, corn flowers, scented rose petals, clover, buddleia flowers, sweet peas
- Small squares of muslin 3 inches square
- Small pieces of dried orange/lemon peel
- Small bay leaf
- Thin piece of ribbon or twine
- Two large sheets of blotting paper or extra thick quality kitchen roll
- Heavy object for weighting/pressing the flowers, such as a pile of books
- Scissors
- Square template
- Name tags

Aim/concept

To help children develop their sensory awareness, by selecting and identifying summer flowers which are suitable for making scented pouches.

Process

- Ask the children to look for flowers in and around their immediate environment, smelling their perfume and noting favourites.
- Explain the importance of removing only a few of the heads, in order that other people can enjoy them, the plants have a chance to make seeds for next year, and insects can continue to visit them for food.
- Permission will be needed from appropriate persons before blooms are picked.
- Remind the children not to pull up or pick the plants of wild flowers, as some are extremely rare.
- Supervise the children as they place the petals/flower heads, orange/lemon peel, and a bay leaf, between two sheets of blotting paper/kitchen roll, spaced apart. Place under a heavy object until they are dry (at least a week).
- Talk about the different shapes, colours and scents of their pressed flowers. Where did they find them?

To make the pouches once flowers are dried

- Using the template, supervise the children in marking and/or cutting out a square from the muslin. Alternatively provide muslin squares.

- Encourage the children to take a selection of dried flowers from the collection and to place them in the centre of the muslin square.
- Discuss the differences observed in looks and smells.
- Bring all four corners together and tie securely with either the ribbon or twine (adult assistance will be required). Name tag the pouches.

Vocabulary/discussion

- Name the different flowers and talk about where they were found: in garden, field, hedgerow, wasteland, and so on.
- Discuss their individual shapes, colours, number of petals, etc.
- Encourage creative language in describing their individual scents.
- Share observations on the insects attracted to the different flowers.

Group size

4–6

Extension ideas

1. Link the activity to a theme/topic on plants/seasons/insects/life processes.
2. Flowers that attract insects usually have a strong scent and can be brightly coloured. Encourage the children to observe and identify the different types of flowers that attract the most insect activity.
3. Discuss the difference between wild and cultivated flowers and their importance and value to the insect world.
4. Decorate name tags with small wild flowers.
5. Use the dried flowers for other creative activities, such as cards or pictures.

Links to Foundation Stage Curriculum

PSE Show care and concern for others, for living things and the environment (SS)

ELG Understand what is right, what is wrong, and why

CLL Talk activities through, reflecting on and modifying what they are doing (SS)

ELG Use talk to organise, sequence and clarify thinking, ideas, feelings and events

KUW Describe simple features of objects and events (SS)

ELG Investigate objects and materials by using all of their senses as appropriate

CD Work creatively on a large or small scale (SS)

ELG Explore colour, texture, shape, form and space in two or three dimensions

Health and safety

⚠ Adult/child awareness of poisonous plants/flowers, such as foxglove (see page 6 for examples).
⚠ Children to wash hands after picking flowers.

ACTIVITY 24   Summer potato and bean harvest

Resources

- Tools for potato digging (trowels/fork)
- Containers for collecting potatoes and beans
- Cooking utensils and provision, i.e. plates, cutlery, saucepans, colander
- A little salt to add to the cooking process (optional)
- A simple recipe if desired
- A measure/ruler

Aim/concept

To enable children to share in the whole group achievement of producing their own crop of beans and potatoes. Digging/picking, collecting, preparing, cooking and eating these vegetables will further add to their enjoyment and give real meaning to this creative 'hands-on' learning experience.

Process

Potatoes

- Remind the children that potatoes are ready for harvesting when the flowers have died and the plant has wilted a little.
- When the signs are right, supervise them as they carefully remove the soil from around the plant using their hands.
- Share in their excitement as they discover the potatoes hidden beneath (they should be about the size of a hen's egg).
- Ask them to collect all the potatoes and place them in the container, counting and smelling them as they do.
- A final dig with a trowel or fork should loosen the plant enough to remove it where further potatoes may be attached to its roots.
- Encourage the children to delve down for any hidden ones.
- Children will love washing the potatoes before boiling them until tender (about 15 minutes). No need to peel new potatoes.

French or kidney beans

- Encourage the children to measure the beans. French beans are ready when about 4 inches in length, and kidney beans when about 8 inches (pick them when they are young and tender).
- Show the children how to pick them. To avoid damaging or pulling at the stem, hold it firmly with one hand and pull the pod downwards with the other. (Extra adult assistance may be needed to help them with this.)
- Ask them to pick only what they need, explaining that new beans will continue to grow for picking on another day.
- Discuss with the children how the vegetables are to be prepared and cooked. If French beans, rinsing in cold water and cooking in boiling water until tender is all that is needed. Kidney beans will need to be sliced first (adult activity), using either a sharp vegetable knife or a special bean slicer (adult supervision needed here), a small gadget especially made for the job. Drain, serve and celebrate with the children in this wonderful organic feast!

Vocabulary/discussion

- Discuss how the vegetables are to be cooked.
- Share in the sensory experience of picking/digging, preparing and tasting the vegetables. How do they smell? What do they feel like?
- How many potatoes were collected from one plant? How many beans have they picked?
- Discuss the different ways potatoes can be cooked.
- Discuss the differences between raw and cooked food.

Group size

4–6

Extension ideas

1. Link the activity to a topic on food, hygiene, health or seasons.
2. Read *Oliver's Vegetables* by Vivian French (Hodder Children's Books).
3. Revisit with the children the whole process of how growing the beans first began (see Activity 16, page 60).
4. Leave a few beans on the stem to dry. Children can then remove the bean from the pod, which they will recognise as the seed from which a new plant can grow for next year.
5. Provide child-friendly cookery books for those children who may wish to explore other methods of cooking fresh vegetables.
6. Discuss the length and weight of the produce.

Links to Foundation Stage Curriculum

CLL	Build up vocabulary that reflects their interests and experiences (SS)
ELG	Extend their vocabulary, exploring the meanings and sounds of new words
MD	Find the total number of items in two groups by counting all of them (SS)
ELG	Begin to relate addition to combining two groups of objects and subtraction to 'taking away'
KUW	Examine objects and living things to find out more about them (SS)
ELG	Find out about, and identify, some features of living things, objects and events they observe
PD	Engage in activities requiring hand–eye coordination (SS)
ELG	Handle tools, objects, construction and malleable materials safely and with increasing control

Health and safety

⚠ Check any child allergies before activity.
⚠ Ensure children wash their hands after digging and picking the produce.
⚠ Adult supervision needed if using bean slicer.
⚠ Adult only to cut and boil vegetables.

Photocopiable pages

Name _____   Date _____

Can you find four different leaves to stick here?

Name _____   Date _____

Name _____   Date _____

Can you find four different flower petals to stick here?

Can you match the trees to their seeds?

Name _____ **Date** _____

A sequencing sheet: Planting a bulb

Draw a line from picture to picture to show the correct order for planting the bulb.

Name _____ **Date** _____

A sequencing sheet:
The 'cycle' of a tree – acorn to oak

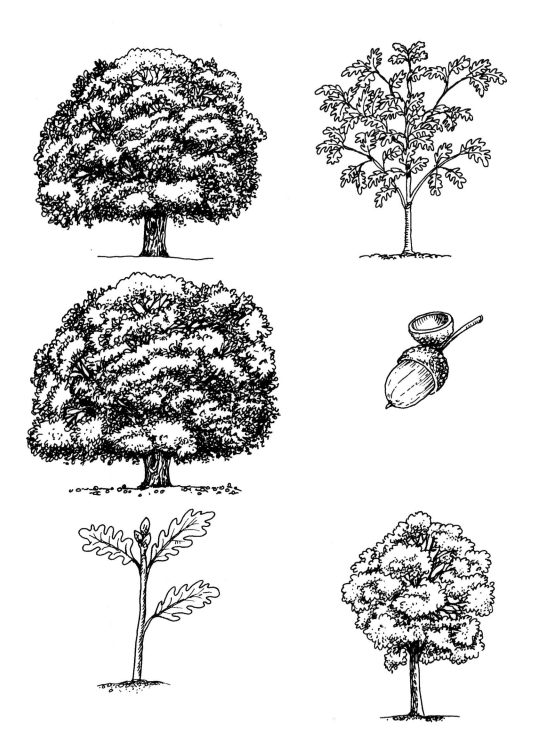

Draw a line from picture to picture to show the growth cycle of the oak tree.

Name _____ **Date** _____

'Rosa's treasure game': The story
(links to Activity 21 on page 72)

Rosa woke up feeling very excited, because today she was going to visit her grandma. Grandma was very special to Rosa and so was her garden. It went on for ever and ever, or so it seemed to Rosa, and as Grandma was very old, she sometimes found it difficult to keep it tidy. It was a wild and wonderful place to explore.

The day was warm and sunny and Grandma said, 'Why don't you take the picnic rug down to the bottom of the garden where it is nice and cool under the trees, and I'll bring the tray out with some lemonade and your favourite muffins.'

Rosa spread the rug out under the old apple tree and lay down. Looking up through the branches, she felt something sticking into her back. Pushing her hand underneath, she felt something rough and pointy. What could it be? Ah, it's a **Stone**, a strange-looking stone. It's got funny patterns on it. She put it in her pocket and lay down again. Spreading her arms out to the side she felt something rough and knobbly. What is it? Ah, a piece of fallen **Bark** from the old apple tree.

'How did that come to fall off?' she thought, as she looked up to the birds singing noisily in the trees. Suddenly something caught her eye, it was floating down towards her. What could it be? Ah, a beautiful soft **Feather**. She caught it in her hand and wondered what bird it had come from.

Rosa became very curious about other things that might be hidden in the garden and decided to explore a bit further to see if she could find other 'treasures'. As she crept quietly through the trees, something snapped under her foot. Bending down, she picked up a **Twig** and then moving forward, she found a **Pine cone**. It was a beautiful shape, but how did it get there? Grandma didn't have any pine trees in her garden. Suddenly something caught her eye. Moving forward she saw something white that she didn't recognise. Rosa picked it up, it was a funny shape. She realised that it was a **Bone**, but from what, where did it come from? Oh and look, a piece of **Fur**. What has happened here? Rosa moved on further to the edge of the garden, where she could just see the fence, and on the floor, what looked like a **Chocolate wrapper** and a **Crisp packet**. Where would these things have come from? It couldn't be Grandma, Grandma would have put them in the bin. But then Rosa had her answer: over the other side of the fence, walking along the pavement, a boy was drinking from a **Can**. He suddenly stopped, screwed it up in his hand and threw it over the fence into Grandma's garden.

'Hey,' shouted Rosa, but he was gone and didn't hear her. She picked up the rubbish and collected all her 'treasures' together, just as Grandma was coming down the garden path.

'Look Grandma, look what I've found,' she said.

Useful contact details and resources

Wiggly Wigglers – For gardening, wildlife ponds, natural pest control and composting.
Tel 01981 500391   www.wigglywigglers.co.uk

The Garden Bird Feeding Guide – Organic gardeners and wildlife products.
Tel 01939 232233   www.gardenbird.com

Duchy Originals HDRA Organic Gardens for Schools Network.
Tel 02476 308217   www.schoolsorganic.net

Insect Lore – Nature and science products for children.
Tel 01908 563338   www.insectlore.co.uk

Waldorf Toys – Modelling beeswax.
www.waldorf-toys.com

Children's Gardening Range at ASDA – Child-sized tools, equipment, seeds, etc. To find your nearest store, contact Customer Services.
Tel 0500 100055   www.asda.com

FACE – Farming and Countryside Education – Helping young people to learn more about food and farming.
Tel (Helpline) 02476 858261   www.face-online.org.uk

Reading suggestions

Nick Butterworth and Mark Inkpen, *Jasper's Beanstalk* (Hodder & Stoughton)

Chiara Chevallier, *The Secret Life of Trees* (Dorling Kindersley Eyewitness Readers, Level 2)

Vivian French, *Oliver's Vegetables* (Hodder Children's Books)

Dyn Sheldon and Gary Blythe, *The Garden* (Hutchinson Children's Books)

Judy Tatchell, *Bugs and Slugs* (Uborne Left-the-Flap Books)

Traditional, *Jack and the Beanstalk*

Catherine Walters, *When Will It Be Spring?* (Magi Publications)

Gabrielle Woolfitt, *Autumn* (Wayland)